LOONS

S0-AVF-136

LOONS

Aubrey Lang and Wayne Lynch

KEY PORTER  BOOKS

DEDICATION

To Flo
who has always encouraged us
in whatever we chose to do

Copyright © 2000 by Key Porter Books

All rights reserved. No part of this work covered by the copyrights hereon may
be reproduced or used in any form or by any means—graphic, electronic or
mechanical, including photocopying, recording, taping or information storage
and retrieval systems—without the prior written permission of the publisher, or
in the case of photocopying or other reprographic copying, a license from the
Canadian Copyright Licensing Agency.

Canadian Cataloguing in Publication Data available on request.

The Canada Council | Le Conseil des Arts
FOR THE ARTS | DU CANADA
SINCE 1957 | DEPUIS 1957

The publisher gratefully acknowledges the support of the Canada Council for
the Arts and the Ontario Arts Council for its publishing program.

We acknowledge the financial support of the Government of Canada through
the Book Publishing Industry Development Program (BPIDP) for our publishing
activities.

Key Porter Books Limited
70 The Esplanade
Toronto, Ontario
Canada M5E 1R2

www.keyporter.com

Printed and bound in China

00 01 02 03 04 05 6 5 4 3 2 1

Preceding page: A common loon incubates its eggs.

CONTENTS

CHAPTER ONE

My most vivid memory of a loon was when I was on a
canoe trip in northern Quebec. It had rained for three days, my
gear was wet and even my spirits were soggy. On the morning of the
fourth day, I got up before sunrise and the storm had passed. I took
my coffee with me to a point overlooking the lake, to watch the day
begin. A thick mist hung over the water and as the sun broke through
the spruce trees, the mist was transformed into an amber veil. A pair of
common loons surfaced near me, leaving a wake of golden threads
trailing behind them. I wanted them to call and when their yodel
echoed across the water, I knew the day would be perfect.

The loon—its elegant look, its mournful call, and its wilderness haunts—
combine to create a powerful wildlife symbol. Sixty million years ago when
the first loon called, its voice reverberated across a swamp filled with strange
creatures that have now disappeared from the face of the earth. Today, when
we hear the ghostly wail of a loon on a northern lake, it awakens something
primeval and sends shivers running down the spine.

Loons have never been so popular. In 1988, schoolchildren voted the common loon as Ontario's official provincial bird. The common loon is also the
state bird of Minnesota. As the loon craze has spread across the continent,
the clothing industry and various other industries have responded with a
whole spectrum of loon paraphernalia. Now, when you pine for the
wilderness, you can even listen to your favorite loon song on the stereo.

In the northern United States, a volunteer network of "loon-watchers" has
been organized to keep track of loons and observe their habits. There is also a
movement called "loon-love" for those who have fallen under the magical
spell of the loon. For others, the loon has become a symbol of love because
loons mate for life.

TALL TALES

Loons are what legends are made of. The loon, more than any other bird, has
repeatedly captured people's imagination. An aura of mystery has always
surrounded this bird. It can appear and disappear like a ghost on water. It
screams its presence with a loud eerie call that makes your hair stand on end,
yet the bird is secretive in its ways and is not easily followed.

Over centuries, the loon has inspired many tales . . . tales about how the
loon created the earth with mud and how the bird acquired its plumage; how

*Opposite: This arctic loon is almost
identical to the pacific loon, with its
grey head and checkered back with
white vertical stripes on the neck.
The arctic loon can be distinguished
by the greenish sheen to its throat.*

it got its call, and how it came to live in water. As the legends circulated among various native peoples—the Inuit, Cree, Ojibwa and Micmac—the stories acquired a distinct regional flavor.

Some legends extolled the supernatural powers of loons. In Siberia, shaman used loons and incantations to travel to the world of spirits. In Mongolia, people believed that after they died they were reincarnated as loons. The skulls of loons have been found in ancient Inuit graves, perhaps placed there to guide the departed soul to the land of spirits. And as recently as the early part of this century, people in Scotland still believed that red-throated loons accompanied souls to heaven.

At various times loons have been considered sacred. In Siberia, misfortune would befall anyone who killed a loon or destroyed its eggs.

The loon was also sacred in parts of Japan, where fishermen used arctic and red-throated loons to guide them in fishing. In 1931, Japanese fishermen even erected a national monument to pay tribute to these birds.

Finally, the Norwegians, and many other cultures, believed that loons could predict the weather; and still today the belief is strong, especially among coastal peoples.

LOON ANCESTRY

As many as 150 million years ago lived the first bird-like creature, *Archeopteryx*; and it was as much a reptile as it was a bird. *Archeopteryx* was the model from which birds evolved. Over eons, birds developed better bodies for flight, and flight allowed birds to settle new habitats that were being created by an ever-changing world.

Scientists have looked back in time to see how birds evolved since *Archeopteryx*. From the fossils they have unearthed, they have come up with 1,760 species of ancient birds. Of those species, 850 are still living today, and one of them is the loon. The loon is very special, not only because it has survived, but because it is the oldest of all living bird species of which there are approximately 9,000 in existence today.

The loon is the first bird you encounter when you open any North American field guide to the birds, since field guides always have the birds in order of the most primitive to the most modern. When we say primitive we tend to think in terms of outdated or unsophisticated, but such is not the case with the loon. As the Roman statesman and author Cicero summed it up two thousand years ago, "Those things are better which are perfected by nature than those which are finished by art." The loon is a survivor, a bird of our times.

THE LOON FAMILY

The loon belongs to the family *Gaviidae* and within this family there are five species of loons: the common loon (*Gavia immer*), the red-throated loon (*Gavia stellata*), the yellow-billed loon (*Gavia adamsii*), the arctic loon (*Gavia arctica*) and the pacific loon (*Gavia pacifica*).

Loons are found in the Northern Hemisphere around the world, and we are fortunate to have all five species nesting in North America. Most people are familiar with the common loon because it nests in the northern United States and throughout Canada. The other four species of loons are found farther north during the nesting season.

THE LOON LOOK

Loons are also called divers, an appropriate name for birds that dive to record depths. They feed primarily on fish and other aquatic life and capture their food on extended dives. Loons ride low on the surface because they have heavier bones than most birds; and their body is long, broad and not very high, features that give them stability on the water. Because all loons are distinguished by a sleek velvety head, a dramatic red eye, and a pointed bill, there is little chance you will mistake a loon for a duck.

The five species of loons vary in weight from three pounds (red-throated) to over fourteen pounds (yellow-billed), with a wingspan of forty-two to fifty-eight inches. The wings appear large, but considering the heavy body they must lift they are relatively small.

In breeding plumage all of the loons are striking. The common loon and the yellow-billed loon are similar with their checkered backs, white on black, and their dark green velvety heads with a patch of white linear markings on their necks. The common loon has a black bill and the yellow-billed is named for its bill.

Distinctive among loons is the red-throated loon. This small loon has a dark grey head, with white linear markings on its nape, a red throat patch and a plain uncheckered back.

The arctic loon and pacific loon are almost identical. Up until 1985, in fact, they were considered the same species. As a result of Russian field studies, the circumpolar population of arctic loons was split into two species: the pacific loon ranging across the North American arctic, and the arctic loon ranging primarily across the Eurasian arctic, although it is also found in Alaska. Both the pacific loon and the arctic loon have a grey head and a checkered back with white vertical stripes on the neck. The subtle difference can be seen in the coloring of the throat. The arctic loon has a greenish sheen to its throat, whereas the pacific loon has a purplish sheen.

All loons have short tails and white underparts which are quite visible when the birds roll on their sides to preen. And all loons have a separate winter plumage which is much less striking than their breeding plumage. In winter plumage, the different species may look quite similar. Basically, the winter plumage of all loons is dark grey above and white below.

Loons' legs are positioned far back on their bodies; too far back to walk like some ducks, yet not quite far enough to allow them to stand erect like a penguin. Their large webbed feet serve as powerful propellers under water. On land loons move awkwardly, rarely coming ashore except to nest.

Two loons swim across a tranquil lake on a misty morning.

A red-throated loon is reflected in the
still waters of Camden Bay, Alaska.

This pacific loon can be distinguished from the arctic loon by the purple sheen on its throat.

Loons feed primarily on fish and other aquatic life and capture their food on extended dives.

Two red-throated loons float on the stillness of a lake.

Loons have a wingspan of forty-two
to fifty-eight inches, and can weigh
up to fourteen pounds.

Although very similar in appearance to the yellow-billed loon, this common loon can be distinguished by its black beak.

Loons have large webbed feet that serve as powerful propellers under water.

The common loon's wings appear large, but considering the heavy body they must lift, they are relatively small.

Loons ride low on the surface because they have heavier bones than most birds.

The plumage of this yellow-billed loon, like the common loon, is striking, with its checkered back, dark green head and white linear markings.

Opposite: In the summer, loons take advantage of a rich food supply and good nesting habitat by migrating to northern lakes.

A red-throated loon sits half-hidden by grass.

An arctic loon swims alone in the chill waters of a northern lake.

Above: A red-throated loon sits on a nest, ever alert for potential predators.

Overleaf: This sheltered spot near the lake's edge would make a fine nesting site.

*An arctic loon searches for food near
a lake's edge.*

A red-throated loon has made its nest in a grassy sanctuary in the middle of a lake.

CHAPTER TWO

I once spent three exciting months sailing around the
Baja Peninsula amidst whales, seabirds and porpoises. Yet, the
day I saw a loon at sea, a rush of emotions overcame me and I
suddenly felt homesick. The loon so typifies the northern wilderness
that on that day, in my reverie, I could see a long-legged moose
wading in the shallows, and a flock of Canada geese wedging across
the sky. I could hear the flap of a beaver's tail on a tranquil
pond and the howl of a wolf on a moonlit night. At that
moment, the loon again exercised its magnetism as the great
spirit of the north and heartened me with its call.

MIGRATION

The regular movement of birds between their summer breeding grounds and
their wintering area is what we call migration. Loons migrate to take advantage of good living conditions. They spend the winter on coastal seas. If they
stayed there throughout the summer, they would be competing with resident
birds for food at a time when they need an abundant food supply to raise
their young. In the summer, loons migrate to northern lakes to take advantage of a rich food supply and good nesting habitat.

The long hours of daylight in the north allow more time for the necessities
of life. During the summer, a loon has to find a territory, attract a mate, build
a nest, incubate the eggs, and raise the young. A great amount of energy is
spent during the reproductive cycle, and the loons have to offset this energy
loss by eating more. Again, the long hours of daylight in the north allow
them more time to feed.

Loons (except the red-throated loon) need open water for take off. They
must leave their breeding grounds before the lakes freeze up or risk getting
trapped by the ice. Loons head south to spend the winter at sea along the
coast. The common loon particularly prefers the more protected areas such
as inlets, bays and coves.

Immature birds spend several years on the ocean before they migrate north
for the first time. Generally, immatures will not return to summer breeding
grounds until they are about three years old and ready to breed, although
there are exceptions. Immature birds need less food than breeding adults and
they are able to compete with resident birds.

*Opposite: Loons are swift and
powerful in flight, as this yellow-
billed loon demonstrates.*

HEADING NORTH

Timing for the migration north is synchronized with the spring thaw on northern lakes. But how do loons know when to head north? And where do they tune in for weather reports on conditions up north? There are probably several factors that influence their timing, but we still do not know exactly what these are. It is known, however, that the "photoperiod"—the number of hours of daylight—influences all temperate and arctic migrating birds. As spring approaches, the brain of the loon senses the increase in day length and this in turn stimulates metabolic changes that prepare it for migration. The final cues which send any bird north still elude us.

Loons that winter the farthest south in coastal Mexico are the first to head north in late March. They frequently fly north along coastal routes until they reach the northern part of the United States where they head inland, and it is probably these loons which nest in the southern end of the bird's range. Loons that winter farther north along the coast leave their wintering grounds in late May or early June and head directly inland, and these loons probably occupy the northern areas of the bird's range. The loons that winter in the Gulf of Mexico fly inland across the central United States.

HEADING SOUTH

Loons tend to leave their breeding grounds in late summer. At the end of each breeding season, pair bonds disintegrate temporarily and loon families split up. Juvenile loons group with their peers, and adults form their own groups, but the members of a breeding pair do not necessarily leave together. As they head south most of the loons form into groups of twenty or more.

En route they stop to rest and feed on large lakes and along the seashore. The Great Lakes are a popular stop for migrants, and some may even stay there through the winter.

Except when they are in breeding pairs, migration is the only time that loons feed together. In winter, loons can be found along the coast in groups or alone. During the day, each loon defends a small feeding territory close to shore, but at night they regroup in deeper waters.

SALT GLANDS

Birds cannot excrete salt through their kidneys as well as mammals can, so birds that drink salt and overload their systems have evolved an alternate way of getting rid of the salt. Loons and other seabirds have very specialized salt glands located above their eyes. Excess salt, absorbed by the bloodstream, is transferred to these glands. The salt glands excrete a very concentrated salt solution into the bird's nasal cavity, and it accumulates in the tip of the bill.

MOLTING

In all birds, feathers wear out and need to be replaced. The adult loon molts and replaces its feathers twice every year. The most important molt occurs when the loons are on their ocean wintering grounds. Before the loons head north they molt and grow their attractive breeding plumage. This molt takes thirty to forty-five days, during which time the loons are flightless. The second molt occurs after the nesting season, but where and when the second molt occurs varies.

Loons that nest in the most northern latitudes, where the summer season is short, have little time to raise their young and little time also to molt. These birds usually molt soon after they return to their wintering grounds, or during migration while they are temporarily stopped on large bodies of water such as the Great Lakes. In more southern latitudes, eg., Minnesota, loons have more time before freeze-up and these birds often shed their old feathers and grow a new set before they migrate.

FEATHER CARE

Sales of down clothing, such as windbreakers, pants and booties, confirm that people value feathers just as much as the birds do.

Feathers provide birds with protection against rain, sleet, cold weather and the harsh rays of the sun. They also serve an aerodynamic function by giving the bird's body a smooth contour which reduces drag in the air. And feathers play an important part in attracting a mate. To fulfill all of these functions, feathers need constant care and indeed the loon, like all birds, spends a great deal of time looking after its feathers.

When preening, the loon grasps a feather at its base and works the feather all the way to the tip, removing oil, dirt and parasites. The bill repositions the feathers and straightens out the barbs on either side of the shaft to provide a smooth, weatherproof coat.

Loons, like most water birds, have a large oil gland on top of the base of their tail. The bird collects the oil with its beak and spreads it over the feathers to keep them water-repellent and supple.

Showers are also part of the routine in maintaining feathers. To shower, loons rise out of the water and splash with their wings. They usually end with a vigorous body shake which settles all of the feathers in their proper places.

With their webbed feet, powerful leg muscles, dense plumage and large oil glands, loons have adapted very well to aquatic life.

Late afternoon consultation.

*Northern bog tundra, summer home
for arctic loons.*

At ease on the nest.

This red-throated loon has chosen a nest well hidden in the shore grasses.

This common loon still carries the grey feathers of a juvenile.

A common loon rushing across the water in a show of aggression.

A nest guarded by a common loon.

Opposite: Standing on the water, a common loon surveys its territory.

Above: Loons, like most water birds, have an oil gland that they use to keep their feathers waterproof and supple.

A common loon moving quickly on the surface of the water.

A family outing.

Opposite: A social group of adult
common loons.

Above: A juvenile common loon,
near Monterey, California.

*A pond in a spruce forest affords a
likely nesting area for loons.*

Loons, like aeroplanes, take a considerable time to become airborne.

*Sunrise on Rain Lake, Algonquin
Park, Ontario.*

Yellow-billed loons are aptly named for their yellow bills.

Opposite: There is nothing more
haunting than the sound of a loon
across a northern lake.

Above: The black and white
checkered back and white necklace
are easily visible on this common
loon.

Chapter Three

My loon memories are interlaced with memories of sunlit shores,
sparkling water and flowering plants. I delight in recalling how
softly the evenings came in the land of the loon. The lapping of
water, the breeze in the trees, and the rhapsodies of streams are the
soothing and restorative sounds of nature that impart a quiet
to the mind and induce a deep sleep.

When the sun beats bright on northern lakes and melts the ice away, the common loon breaks the silence of winter, arriving to breed. Warm weather and longer hours of daylight stir the birds into reproductive behavior.

HOME SWEET HOME
Almost all species of birds, at some time, establish and defend an area called a territory, which is usually defended against individuals of their own kind. Loons establish a territory during breeding time in order to have exclusive use of an area for mating, nesting, feeding and raising their young.

Common loons establish or reoccupy their territories soon after the lakes thaw. Without open water, the loons are unable to land; therefore loons nesting farther north arrive on their breeding grounds much later than their southern counterparts. In New Hampshire, for example, loons may be on territory in April, while in northern Alberta the loons may not arrive until the middle of May. Farther north they arrive even later. Where the summer season is short, loons waste no time getting started on nesting activities.

Loons mate for life but they don't necessarily spend the winter together. A question then arises. How does a pair of loons find each other in the vast northern expanses, year after year? The answer is that loons usually return to the same territory and sometimes to the same nesting site of their first breeding season. This behavior is called "site fidelity."

Male birds tend to arrive first and the females soon join them, but in years when the ice is late to melt, loons may join up with their mates before they reach the territory in "waiting areas" of open water. Some couples mate during this time and finally get to their territories when the ice has melted. Once established, the birds advertise and defend their territories with various calls and visual displays. In some years when lakes are slow to thaw, loons may not even attempt to nest as they would not have enough time to raise their young before the lakes froze over.

Opposite: Loons prefer to nest where they have easy access to water, if danger threatens.

Loon territories vary in size. Nesting lakes can be large or small, and the water can be deep or shallow, but loons seem to prefer a territory that has both deep and shallow water. Lakes that range from 100–200 acres usually support only one pair of loons, unless there are land features on the lake that provide enough privacy for another pair to raise their young. Larger lakes often support several breeding pairs.

SOCIAL GROUPS

There is a population of nonbreeding loons that spends the summer on lakes throughout the breeding grounds. These birds are nonbreeders because they either do not have a mate, or because they have not found a suitable territory. Some of these birds may be simply too young to breed. The nonbreeders cruise the waters, often close to occupied territories; and should a territory become vacant, it is quickly taken over by one of these birds.

Throughout the summer, nonbreeders gather in groups, usually in the early morning and evening. These groups are often joined by one or both members of a breeding pair. As the season progresses, and loon chicks become more independent, both parents spend increasing amounts of time with the group. For breeding pairs, these social gatherings help ease the transition from territorial life to winter group life.

COURTSHIP

Loons give showy and noisy displays that are delightful to watch, but these displays usually express aggression and they should not be mistaken for displays of affection. Courtship displays, on the other hand, are more subtle. After the birds arrive on a territory, they spend time feeding and preening together. They swim along the shore, side by side, turning their heads, dipping their bills, and submerging their heads. Eventually the male goes to shore and calls for the female to follow. The call sounds like a soft "mew." The female may or may not follow right away, but she eventually succumbs to his call. The male mounts her from behind, on land, and the copulation may last anywhere from three to ten minutes. When he is done he walks up her back, over her head, and into the water. The female may also initiate copulation by calling the male to shore.

NESTING

Sometimes the pair will nest where they mated, but many factors affect the final selection of a nest site. A good spot offers easy access to the water, and is even better if the water is deep enough to dive into. This way, if danger threatens, the loon can immediately dive and surface away from the nest, keeping the nest location a secret.

Loons prefer to nest on islands where mammalian predators are less likely to discover the eggs, and a site that offers overhead cover protects the eggs from avian predators. They ideally select a nest site that offers a good view of the territory, and one that is protected from the wind. Strong winds (and also motorboats) can generate swells that can flood an unprotected nest.

What all nests have in common is that they are located next to the water. You may even find nests on half-submerged logs, mats of rotting vegetation, and on top of abandoned muskrat houses.

For nest building, loons use a variety of materials: grasses, reeds, muck from the lake bottom, cattails, twigs, leaf litter, moss and whatever else is handy. If no nesting materials are available, they simply lay their eggs on bare rock or in the sand.

If water levels rise, most loons will build up the nest to keep their eggs above the water. If the water level drops, however, the loon is left "high and dry." In this case it has to shuffle over land to reach the nest, and since it moves about so poorly on land it may eventually abandon the nest.

EGG LAYING

Loons normally lay two eggs, and the eggs of all species are remarkably similar in appearance, usually large, olive-brown, with dark spots and blotches. Loons incubate their eggs for about thirty days, with the male and female taking turns sitting on the nest. Every time they relieve each other from egg-sitting duty (usually every two to three hours), the arriving loon turns the eggs.

The eggs usually hatch within twenty-four hours of each other. At hatching, chicks weigh just a few ounces, yet their eyes are open and they are fully alert. Soon afterwards, the dark brown, fluffy chicks leave the nest and the parents lead them to a protected area of shallow water, where there are small fish on which to feed. Both adults catch the fish to feed the baby loons.

PREDATORS

The egg stage is a vulnerable time, and the adults are on the nest ninety-nine percent of the time. Each year, eggs disappear from loon nests, often without a trace. Predation by ravens and eagles may explain many mysteriously empty loon nests. Ravens have such large beaks that they are able to carry off whole loon eggs, and more incriminating, loon eggs have been found in raven nests. In other cases, scientists have been able to identify other culprits. In the Arctic, parasitic jaegers, herring gulls and arctic foxes are the main predators.

Farther south, wherever the ranges of the raccoon and the common loon overlap, the raccoon is a likely predator. In New Hampshire, raccoons destroy many nests, and in some years, they have destroyed seventy-five to eighty percent of all the nests on the state's two largest lakes.

Herring gulls are large aggressive gulls that frequently prey on both loon eggs and chicks. In northern Ontario, I once saw a herring gull carry off a loon chick that had been left alone while its parents were fishing.

In the boreal forest and in the coastal areas, bald eagles and common loons often nest on the same secluded northern lakes. I have watched eagles harass swimming loons by swooping on them, and other observers have reported seeing eagles carry off loon chicks.

Skunks, foxes and mink have also been found guilty of raiding the nests of loons.

In addition, people may inadvertently threaten a loon nest. When they approach too closely, the incubating bird will normally slip off the nest, thus leaving the unattended eggs vulnerable to sharp-eyed predators.

When the adults fish for themselves, one parent usually stays with the chicks while the other bird goes off to feed. In some cases, when a pair of loons nest on a small lake, there may not be enough fish to feed both the adults and the chicks. Then the adults fly to another lake to feed. If the chicks are left alone, they hide in shallow water close to shore until the parents return.

Besides watching for avian and mammalian predators, parents also frequently peer under the water to check for predators that lurk there. Large fish and turtles can swallow a baby loon in a single gulp. One place that is safe and cozy is mother and father's back. During the first two weeks, the chicks often ride on their parents' backs to rest and to keep warm. At this age, they easily get chilled because down doesn't offer the same thermal protection as adult plumage. At six weeks the chicks lose their down and it is replaced with regular feathers.

The eggs of all loon species are usually large, olive-brown, with dark spots and blotches.

Opposite: All loon nests, like this yellow-billed loon's, are built near the water as loons are unable to walk easily on land.

Above: An arctic loon nest.

This common loon seems to be standing on the water, a feat meant to threaten a rival.

*Loons mate for life, usually returning
to the same nesting territory.*

Above: Sometimes loons nest on half-submerged logs or mats of rotting vegetation.

Opposite: Walking onto the nest must be done carefully to avoid harming the eggs.

Above: This red-throated loon ducks down in its nest.

Opposite: Bathurst Inlet, NWT, is the nesting area of this red-throated loon.

Above: A loon's legs are set so far
back on its body that it moves poorly
on land.

Opposite: In hot summer weather,
loons pant to cool themselves.

*Ideally, a nest site offers a good view
of the territory.*

Loons usually return to the same territory and sometimes to the same nesting site of their first breeding season.

Loons normally lay two eggs and the
eggs of all species are remarkably
similar in appearance.

An arctic loon shows off its splendid stripes.

The male and female share tending the eggs. Each time they relieve each other, the eggs are turned.

Above: If the water level rises, most loons will build up the nest to keep their eggs from getting wet.

Overleaf: Loons incubate their eggs for about thirty days, with male and female taking turns sitting on the nest.

A red-throated loon turns its eggs.

An incubating red-throated loon shows off its colorful neck.

Above: An arctic loon keeps a wary eye out for predators.

Opposite: A loon chick awaits the return of the parent bird.

Newly hatched and still wet.

A young arctic loon takes to the water, head held high.

Opposite: Eagles and ravens prey on loon eggs.

Right: Wherever the ranges of the raccoon and the common loon overlap, the raccoon is a likely predator.

CHAPTER FOUR

It was spring and the morning was dewy and fresh. I sat outside
my tent and waited for the early morning rays to warm my bones.
The air was sweet with the scent of the earth. A fluttering sound
startled me and loons came dashing across the water in front of my
camp. Their yodel echoed for miles as if to herald the dawning of a
new day. I felt whole then and at one with the earth.

FISHY DIET

Loons are primarily fish eaters and they will catch whichever species of fish
they can. They are often accused, unjustly, of depleting a lake of game fish.
However, game fish, such as trout, are difficult for a loon to catch. A trout
swims in a straight line and is capable of quick bursts of speed, allowing it to
stay ahead of the loon. As well, the trout often heads for deeper water where
visibility is poor, and the loon loses sight of it. Loons are more successful at
catching slower fish that zigzag to escape. Loons also feed on crayfish,
aquatic insects and sometimes vegetation. While photographing a common
loon in northern Saskatchewan, photographer Wayne Lynch observed the
bird repeatedly feeding on leeches.

Loons need good visibility to hunt; so they hunt in lakes that have clear
water, and they hunt during the day. They continually peer under water and
when they spot a fish, they dive and chase their prey. They usually catch fish
at depths of six to twelve feet where visibility is good.

Young chicks are fed minnows and other small fish. Parents catch the fish
and stimulate the young to feed by dipping the fish in the water and
splashing. One researcher learned first hand how important this stimulus was
when a captive loon chick refused to eat. After trying every trick in the book
to get the chick to eat, the researcher used the same tactic of dipping and
splashing the fish in front of the young bird, and it worked.

As the chicks get older the parents offer them progressively larger fish, and
eventually the adults give the chicks a chance to develop their own hunting
skills. A parent will drop a fish that is stunned or partly paralysed in front of
the chicks and the young loons chase after it. By six weeks of age, the young
loons are able to catch their own fish, but most of their food is still supplied
by their parents. Over the summer the chicks are left to forage alone for
increasingly longer periods but the parents continue to supplement the young
birds' diet until they are three months old.

Opposite: If the water is too cold, this chick can always ride on one of its parents' back to rest and keep warm.

During the winter when most loons are at sea, they feed close to shore. Each new tide brings in an abundance of food and loons feed on crustaceans and a variety of fish such as sea trout, mackerel, flounder, herring and cod.

BEAKS AND GIZZARDS

As birds evolved, they lost the heavy jaws and teeth that made prehistoric birds "nose-heavy" and awkward in flight. To lighten their load and become better flyers, modern birds evolved a lightweight keratin bill.

A bill is not designed to grind food, so how does a bird break up its food? Birds have gizzards that serve as grinders. The gizzard is a muscular structure that is part of the stomach. It has a hard keratin lining that can pulverize hard shells, bones and vegetable matter with the help of strong, rhythmic contractions. Sometimes, additional grit is used to help grind food in the stomach. Biologist Judy McIntyre has observed loons swallowing gravel, presumably for this purpose.

DIVING

Loons can disappear from the water surface without leaving a ripple and they can travel very quickly underwater. They can dive to depths of 200 feet or more and some fishermen have found them in fishing nets at depths of 265 feet. Their aquatic feats are impressive indeed.

All water birds share special adaptations to aquatic life: webbed feet, powerful leg muscles, dense plumage and large oil glands to waterproof their feathers.

Loons are so well adapted to swimming and diving that they have sacrificed agility on land. Their legs are at the rear of their body and serve as rudders without interfering with the body's streamlining. With their powerful legs and webbed feet, they can "turn on a dime" just by extending a foot to the side. Unlike penguins, loons do not use their wings to swim under water.

Getting below the surface of the water presents a challenge for all diving birds. Most birds have bones that are filled with airspaces because they need a lightweight frame for flight. A lightweight frame on a loon would make it very difficult for the bird to submerge and stay under water, so the loon has evolved denser and heavier bones than most birds. Loons have sacrificed ease in flight for ease in diving. To further reduce buoyancy, loons compress their feathers to force out trapped air just before they dive.

How does the loon manage prolonged dives without a scuba tank? This aspect of loon biology has not been well researched. Experts speculate that the loon has probably developed the same physiological adaptations that are found in other diving birds: a larger than average blood volume, a high concentration of oxygen-carrying hemoglobin in the blood, and a high concentration of oxygen-storing myoglobin in the muscles. These three adaptations increase the oxygen reserves of a diving bird and, in a sense, function like a metabolic scuba tank. Also, diving birds conserve oxygen by diverting blood away from nonvital tissues such as skin. By reducing blood flow to the skin, the loon also loses less body heat during a dive.

The record diving time is five minutes for the arctic loon and three minutes for the common loon, but the average diving time is about forty-two seconds. Loons dive not only to feed, but to escape danger, and diving is used in some displays as part of their sign language.

FLY LIKE A LOON
Loons are swift and powerful in flight but they have trouble getting airborne. The wings have a heavy load to carry and the birds cannot spring immediately into flight. Like aeroplanes, loons have to motor down a runway to get the lift they need, and they also have specialized curved feathers that provide additional lift.

With wings beating at a fast clip, loons may run as far as a quarter of a mile to pick up the speed they need to get aloft. In the air, loons maintain a rapid wingbeat and they can fly at speeds of 75 MPH. Compare this with ducks that fly at speeds of 45–60 MPH.

Besides watching for avian and mammalian predators, parents also frequently peer under the water to check for predators that lurk there.

Young chicks are fed minnows and other small fish.

*This common loon conceals its eggs
from potential predators by lying low
over its nest.*

A common loon sits on a well-hidden nest.

On a warm day, a chick tries to get
some shelter from the sun by sitting
in its parent's shadow.

If loon chicks are left alone, they hide in shallow water close to shore until the parents return.

Opposite: In winter when most loons are at sea, they feed on crustaceans, trout, mackerel, flounder, herring and cod.

Above: Loons have adapted well to the water. Their bodies are streamlined and their legs serve as rudders.

A bill is not designed to grind food,
so birds have gizzards for that
purpose. The gizzard can pulverize
hard shells, bones and vegetable
matter.

*Above: A chick stays near the safety
of its parent.*

*Overleaf: The dense foliage around
this lake provides cover for many
nesting sites.*

A common loon rushes to drive an
intruder from its territory.

Loons need good visibility to hunt, so they hunt in lakes that have clear water. They continually peer under water and when they spot a fish, they dive and chase their prey.

Above: Loon chicks accompany their parents on a swim, and will eventually learn how to catch fish.

Opposite: This chick stays near the familiarity of its nest while its parents are away catching fish.

Opposite: Loons have to protect their
nests from a number of predators,
including raccoons, herring gulls,
bald eagles, skunks, foxes and mink.

Above: When it matures, this fluffy
chick will turn into a replica of its
stately parent.

Preceding Pages: With a parent on either side, the chicks can swim safely on one of their first outings.

Above: Loons have gathered to stake out nesting sites at an Alaskan lake.

Loons have sacrificed ease in flight for ease in diving. To further reduce buoyancy, loons compress their feathers to force out trapped air just before they dive.

*Loons incubate their eggs for about
thirty days.*

Backwaters like this one in Manitoba's Whiteshell Provincial Park are used by loons as nesting sites.

Chicks retain their dark fluffy down until they are six weeks old when the down is replaced with regular feathers.

During the first few months of life, loon chicks are dependent on their parents for food and protection from predators. By six weeks of age, they are able to catch their own fish, but most of their food is still supplied by their parents.

CHAPTER FIVE

I often photograph loons from the water, and when I do,
I wear a black neoprene wet suit. At the height of mosquito season,
I usually top off my outfit with a green mosquito head net. One
evening, as I emerged out of the cattails on to a logging road in
northern Ontario, I nearly caused an accident. The driver of a
logging truck was so startled by what he saw that he almost drove
into the lake. I am sure he thought he had seen an alien.

HOW LOONS COMMUNICATE

With such a well-developed sense of vision and hearing, it is not surprising
that loons use both visual displays and calls to communicate with each other.

The meaning of a certain call or a display is difficult to decipher and may
vary depending on the context in which it is given. Every year, however,
researchers bring new light on the subject. Sonograms, which are printouts of
vocalizations, have helped tremendously in our understanding of how loons
communicate with calls. For example, sonograms have confirmed that each
male loon has its own unique "identity call."

LOON TUNES

Loon calls fall into four categories: "tremolo," "yodel," "wail" and "hoot" —
unflattering names for such a mesmerizing repertoire. These calls carry
messages of love and hate, and they are combined with various postures to
convey different emotions.

The yodel is used exclusively by males, and it serves as the bird's identity
call. The yodel is used with a low "crouch position" in aggressive displays of
low intensity. In situations of extreme aggression, and for encounters of the
close kind, the yodel is used in a raised "vulture position."

The tremolo is an alarm call used when the bird or its young are threatened.
Loons may get very agitated, and run across the water to and fro, calling
excitedly. They also use this call when they fly over an occupied territory.

The hoot is a "toot your horn" kind of call used to announce their presence
when approaching other birds, and to keep track of each other.

The wail is apparently the first call uttered by a chick. Parents wail to lure
the chicks away from the nest or to call the chicks to them when they surface
with a fish. Wail calls are used when birds want company, and also when

Opposite: Loons often "dance across the water" as part of a threat display.

they want intimacy; the male wails when he wants to attract the female to shore for mating.

DANCING ON WATER

Visual displays are a type of sign language used by loons to express their moods. The displays, often accompanied by vocalizations, are used in courtship, to reinforce a bond, to express alarm, threaten an intruder, and to advertise or defend a territory.

The objective of a threat display is to produce a frightening effect, forcing an opponent to retreat. To achieve this, a loon may rise out of the water, spread its wings and strike the surface with powerful wing beats. It may also race across the water in this position. Loons have often been filmed "dancing across the water," and invariably the background music used leads the viewer to erroneously believe that this is a dance of romance.

Circling, splash diving and rushing are other displays that show varying degrees of aggression. These displays are used alone, or in a sequence, to show mounting aggression. Just before an outright attack the loon rises into a "vulture position," ready to rush and stab the opponent with its bill. The loon's bill is a formidable weapon that can seriously wound or kill an opponent.

Another visual display is the appeasement display which brings birds closer together. This display inhibits aggression and reinforces the bond between the members of a pair and between parents and young. In an appeasement display the loon makes itself look smaller and less threatening by riding low in the water and by "bill dipping" and turning its head to de-emphasize its menacing bill.

RAIN, RAIN, GO AWAY

The threat of acid rain is no longer a threat but a reality. We continue to burn fossil fuels that pollute the atmosphere, and the pollution returns to the earth as acid rain. Acid rain is destroying the food chain in many northern lakes where loons return year after year to raise their young. When lakes become acidic, fish populations dwindle. When the lakes become very acidic, they cannot sustain life of any kind. Adult loons manage to survive on acidic lakes by flying back and forth to feed on lakes where fish can still be found. Loon chicks, of course, are unable to fly, and they are affected most by increasing lake acidity because they must survive on the lakes where they are born. What was the land of plenty is fast becoming a death trap for loon chicks.

The common loon, whose range overlaps most with that of people and pollution, is the most seriously affected.

SPRAYING THE WORLD TO DEATH

We continually mistreat the environment, the same environment that we share with other forms of life. Now we are forced to clean up our mess because our own survival is being threatened by our carelessness and mismanagement.

For years, we have been using broad-spectrum pesticides (DDT, aldrin, dieldrin) and other substances that remain in the environment for a very long time. These substances contaminate water and soil, and they are spread via water currents and air. DDT has even reached the penguins of the Antarctic region.

Pollutants are concentrated as they move up the food chain, and at each step their deleterious effects are magnified. The species at the top are naturally the most affected. Since the loon is at the top of its food chain, it is vulnerable to the effects of pollutant accumulation.

Insufficient research has been done to determine the side effects of pollutants in loons, but we know how pollutants affect other birds.

Pollutants accumulate in a bird's fat deposits. When the bird is stressed (eg., migration, disease, food shortage) fat deposits are mobilized and large amounts of pollutants are released into the bloodstream, affecting the bird in various ways. Birds may be rendered infertile, or they may lay eggs that contain dead embryos or that have thin, fragile eggshells that are easily crushed. Adults may develop aberrant behaviors such as eating their own eggs. Pollutants may also weaken a bird and cause it to die prematurely.

Industrial wastes, such as mercury, are other pollutants that are dumped into our rivers, lakes and oceans, and endanger our wildlife (and ourselves). Fish absorb methylmercury (the toxic form of mercury) through their gills. Mercury poisoning affects humans, and in many countries, strict standards have been established to control the sale of fish with high mercury levels. Loons, however, have no protection against mercury poisoning and no other source of food.

OIL DAMAGE

Three million tons of oil are spilled into our oceans every year, and oil spills are increasing as our worldwide consumption of oil increases. Oil pollution is not always accidental and our oceans are often used as garbage dumps for oil wastes.

When birds get covered with oil, their feathers lose their insulating quality and the birds are no longer able to stay warm. As well, when they try to remove the oil with their beaks, they inadvertently ingest some of it, and they frequently suffer fatal liver and kidney disease.

After writing the sections on oil slicks, pollutants and industrial wastes, I felt sad because when we destroy our environment, we destroy much of what fuels the human spirit. Every year we spend millions of dollars to preserve our creations. What kind of a legacy are buildings, paintings, sculptures and artifacts? We are so involved with ourselves that we have forgotten nature is the force that shaped the human mind, and nature has always been a source of inspiration. When nature is gone, can our structures inspire works of art, or can we find inspiration on the moon? Human attitudes will determine the future of our environment and the future of loons.

CONCLUSION

I feel privileged to have witnessed many of the great wildlife spectacles of the world: the wildebeest migration in Africa's Serengeti Plains, polar bears on the Arctic pack ice, and the kaleidoscope of bird life in tropical rain forests, deserts and mountains. What I have discovered from all of my travels is that the excitement of observing animals and birds does not lie in exotic settings. The excitement lies in understanding what you see. More simply stated, I enjoy nature when I understand nature. My encounters with loons continue to excite me because of what I have learned about these marvellous birds, about the natural forces that shape them and about the forces that may destroy them. I hope the information in this book will excite you as it has me, and enrich your next encounter with those magnificent birds of the tundra and taiga—the loons.

The common loon is found throughout Canada and the northern United States.

A common loon guards its nest against intruders.

Nature is a source of inspiration. We must work to clean up and preserve the environment for all wildlife.

A red-throated loon prepares to take off.

Above: Loon calls are combined with various postures to convey different emotions.

Overleaf: The sky is reflected in the still waters of Manitoba's Whiteshell Provincial Park, which provides good habitat for loons.

Loons establish a territory during breeding time in order to reserve an area for mating, nesting, feeding and raising their young.

Industrial wastes, such as mercury, are dumped into rivers, lakes and oceans. Loons have no protection against such poisoning.

The appeasement display brings birds
closer together. The loon makes itself
look smaller and less threatening by
riding low in the water.

The objective of a threat display is to force an intruder to retreat.

Opposite: An arctic loon surveys an icy northern lake.

Above: A group of yellow-billed loons enjoy a morning swim.

Opposite: Visual displays are used by
loons to express their moods. In order
to achieve a threat display, this
common loon rises out of the water
and spreads its wings.

Above: A common loon is putting on
a threat display to defend its territory
during the nesting season.

The long hours of daylight in the north allow loons more time for finding a territory for nesting.

Above: Protected areas, such as Rain Lake in Ontario's Algonquin Park, make ideal nesting areas for loons.

Overleaf: A pair of red-throated loons set out to catch fish.

The appeasement display inhibits aggression and reinforces the bond between members of a pair.

Our oceans are often used as garbage dumps for oil wastes. This common loon is soiled with oil from a spill off the California coast.

Loons have well-developed vision and hearing, so they use visual displays and calls to communicate with each other.

Loons prefer nesting lakes that have both deep and shallow water.

Photo Credits

Robert W. Baldwin, 45, 76-77, 102, 111
Glenn R. Davy, 50, 137
C.G. Hampson, 66, 78, 79
Bill Ivy, 70, 114, 143
Edgar T. Jones, 20, 21, 28, 29, 30, 51, 60, 67, 68, 72, 133
Gary R. Jones, 6
Albert Kuhnigk/First Light, 24, 61, 130, 132
Wayne Lynch, 37, 52, 71, 84, 85, 92, 113, 126-27, 141
Sandy MacDonald, 15
Brian Milne/First Light, 14, 23, 38, 63, 97, 98, 124,
   138-39
George K. Peck, 54, 75, 96, 100-101, 140
Mark K. Peck, 3, 46, 62, 83, 115, 131
R. Barry Ranford, 25, 36, 41, 59, 73, 74, 80, 122
Paul Rezendes, 26-27, 71, 136
James M. Richards, 13, 40, 48, 49, 64, 82
Lynn Rogers, 11, 16, 18, 19, 34, 35, 39, 42, 43, 44, 47,
   53, 65, 69, 81, 86, 91, 93, 94, 95, 99, 103, 105, 107,
   108-9, 112, 116, 121, 123, 125, 128, 129, 134, 142
W.E. Ruth, 90, 106
Tom Walker, 12, 22, 110
Terry G. Willis, 17, 135
Harold E. Wilson, 104